TREASURY OF
ART NOUVEAU
DESIGN & ORNAMENT

A Pictorial Archive of 577 Illustrations

Selected by
Carol Belanger Grafton

Dover Publications, Inc.
New York

Published in Canada by General Publishing
Company, Ltd., 30 Lesmill Road, Don Mills,
Toronto, Ontario.
Published in the United Kingdom by Constable
and Company, Ltd., 10 Orange Street, London
WC2H 7EG.

Treasury of Art Nouveau Design and Ornament
is a new work, first published by Dover
Publications, Inc., in 1980.

DOVER *Pictorial Archive* SERIES

Book design by Carol Belanger Grafton

International Standard Book Number: 0-486-24001-0
Library of Congress Catalog Card Number: 80-65964

Manufactured in the United States of America
Dover Publications, Inc.
31 East 2nd Street
Mineola, N.Y. 11501

PUBLISHER'S NOTE

IN the last decade of the nineteenth century and the first decade of the twentieth, an exciting new style appeared in painting, sculpture and architecture, but most especially in the applied arts. This new style, which has come to be called "Art Nouveau," was characterized by a lack of straight lines and an emphasis on fluid movement within compositions. This book is a compendium of Art Nouveau design, taken from the pages of *The Studio, Art et Décoration* and other well-known period publications. Artists represented here include Gustav Klimt, Ethel Larcombe, Will Bradley, George Auriol and other masters of the Art Nouveau style. At the end of this collection is a list which identifies the artists and the publications from which the art derives, accompanied by a bibliography of sources.

Graphic artist and book designer Carol Belanger Grafton has selected these designs and ornaments to be of maximum use to artists and craftspeople. Display type in mastheads, advertisements and bookplates has been retained for its Art Nouveau authenticity. Modern artists may want to eliminate this original type and substitute type of their own.

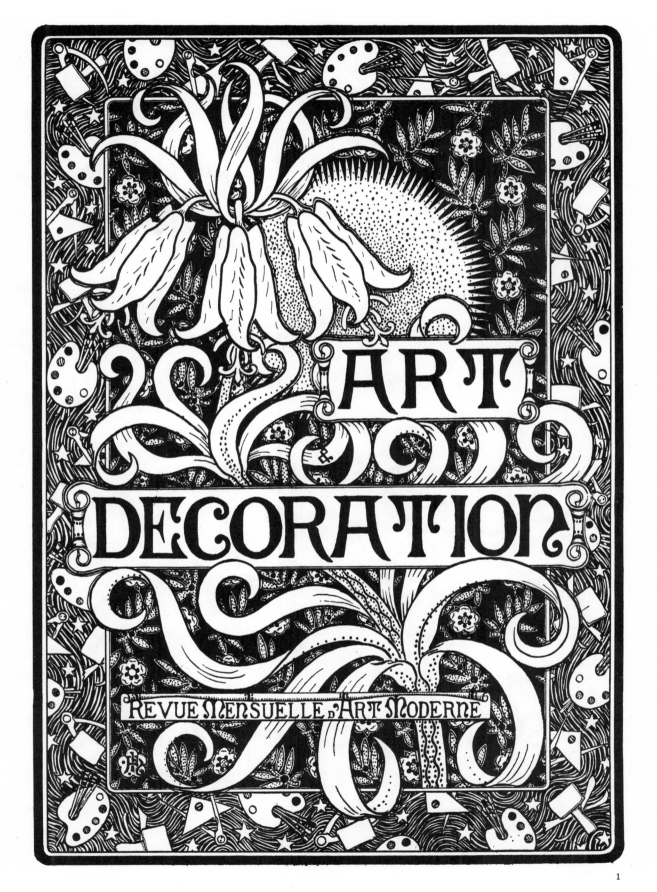

ART
DECORATION
REVUE MENSUELLE D'ART MODERNE

2

THE first VOLUME of the Butterfly

3

4

5

ART ET DECORATION

REVVE . MENSUELLE . ILLUSTREE . D'ART . MODERNE ... PARIS . 13 .
RUE . LAFAYETTE ....

6

7

8

9

EX·LIBRIS

DAVID
ALLEN

10

LIBRI·
VIRESCIT

SEMPER
·AMOR·

11

EX·LIBRIS

12

IN THE KEY OF THE BLUE

13

POEMS BY OSCAR WILDE

14

15

16

17

18

19

20

21

22

23

24

25

26

OLGA VON KASPEROWICZ

27

28

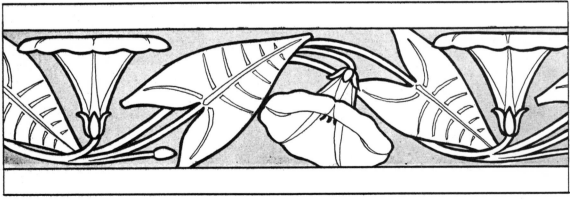

29

8

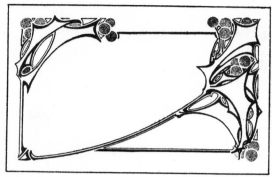

30

31

32

33

34

35

37

38

39

36

10

40

41

43

Plaquettes et Médailles
des maîtres modernes

37ter Quai de l'HORLOGE, PARIS   Téléph 246.10.
A. GODARD . GRAVEUR-ÉDITEUR
UNIQUE DÉPOSITAIRE DES ŒUVRES COMPLÈTES DE
O. ROTY
MEMBRE DE L'INSTITUT

ŒUVRES DE CHAPLAIN, MEMBRE DE L'INSTITUT

Daniel DUPUIS, L. BOTTÉE, F. VERNON, PATEY, G. DUPRÉ, PRUD'HOMME, etc.

Envoi du Catalogue illustré sur demande
Prix : 6 francs

44

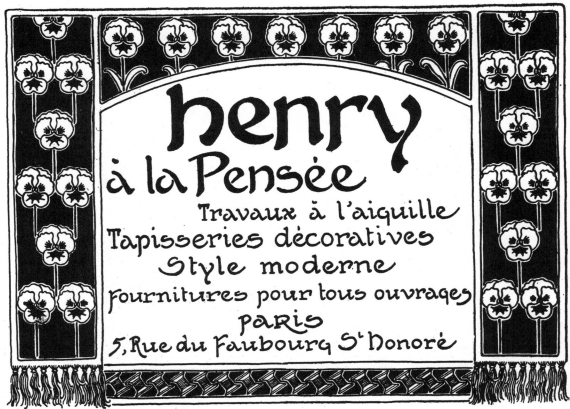

henry
à la Pensée
Travaux à l'aiguille
Tapisseries décoratives
Style moderne
Fournitures pour tous ouvrages
PARIS
5, Rue du Faubourg St Honoré

45

Henry
à la Pensée
Travaux à l'aiguille
Tapisseries décoratives
Style moderne
Fournitures pour tous ouvrages
Médaille d'or à l'exposition
universelle
de 1889.

46

ART NOUVEAU BING
AMEUBLEMENTS
OBJETS D'ART
APPAREILS
D'ÉCLAIRAGE
Ateliers & Magasins
22 Rue
de Provence
PARIS.

47

La Tapisserie

48

49

LE THYRSE
Par
Arnold
Goffin

Charles Vos
Bruxelles

50

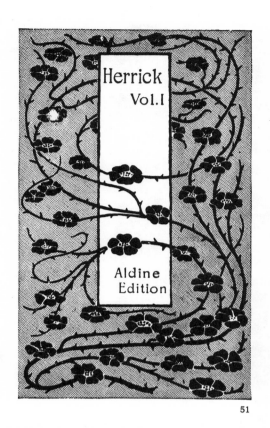

Herrick
Vol. I

Aldine
Edition

51

SIR EDWARD
BURNE-JONES
A RECORD AND
REVIEW

52

53

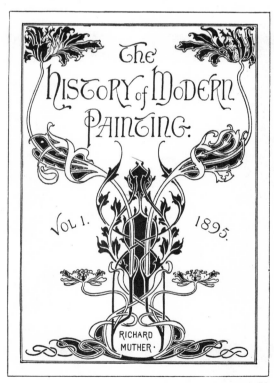

The
HISTORY of MODERN
PAINTING.

VOL I. 1895.

RICHARD
MUTHER.

54

"Under der linden
an der heide·
dâ unser zweier bette was·
dâ muget ir vinden
schône beide
gebrochen bluomen unde gras·
vor dem walde in einem tal·
tandaradei!
schône sanc diu nahtegal·

55

56

57

18

58

59

60

61

62

LE
FONTI
SALVTARI
D'ITALIA

I POETI GRECI

TRADOTTI DA ETTORE ROMAGNOLI

64

Société Philanthropique Française de Berlin

PROGRAMME DE LA SOIRÉE DU 11 Novembre 1905

C-G

65

LE GRASSET

66

LA FONTA-NA · LA LUNA · LE ROSE ·

D. BEVILACQUA

67

68

THE · · ·
LYRICAL
· POEMS
OF · · ·
EDMUND
SPENSER

69

70

71

72

THE STUDIO

PROFUSELY
ILLUSTRATED

AN ILLUSTRATED
MAGAZINE OF FINE
& APPLIED ART

SHOULD BE
READ BY

ARCHITECTS, ARTISTS,
DESIGNERS, STUDENTS
AND ALL LOVERS OF ART.

PRICE
SIXPENCE
MONTHLY.

73

THE STUDIO

AN ILLUSTRATED
MAGAZINE OF
FINE AND APPLIED
ARTS.
PROFUSELY ILLUSTRATED.
SHOULD BE READ BY
ARCHITECTS,
ARTISTS, DESIGNERS,
STUDENTS AND ALL
LOVERS OF ART

PRICE SIXPENCE MONTHLY.

74

75

76

77

78

79

80

81

82

The Studio

AN ILLUSTRATED ᴧᴧᴧᴧ
MAGAZINE of FINE AND
ᴧᴧᴧᴧ APPLIED ARTS

VOL I. LONDON
THE STUDIO OFFICES
16 HENRIETTA ST·COVENT GARDEN

83

ART et DECORATION

revue mensuelle d'art decoratif moderne

Sommaire

84

29

85

86

88

87

89

90

91

92

94

93

PICKFORD WALLER

95

WE·SHOVLD·MAKE·THE·SAME·
VSE·OF·A·BOOK·THAT·THE·BEE·
DOES·OF·A·FLOWER·SHE·STEALS·
SWEETS·FROM·IT·BVT·
DOES·NOT·
INJVRE·
IT·

96

HILDA'S·BOOK·

97

Huon of Bordeaux

98

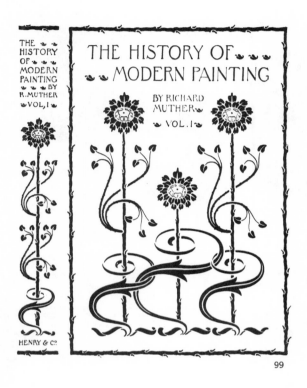

99

100

101

102

103

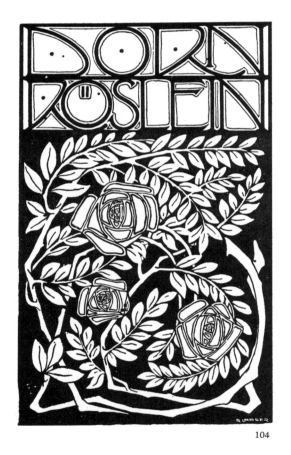

104

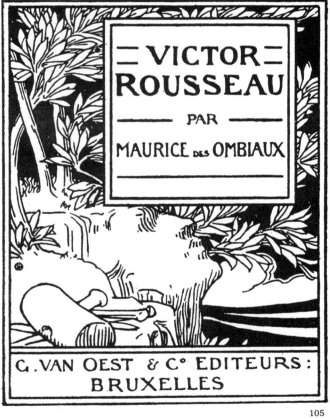

VICTOR ROUSSEAU

PAR

MAURICE des OMBIAUX

G. VAN OEST & C° EDITEURS:
BRUXELLES

105

ORO ALLA PATRIA

106

107

108

109

110

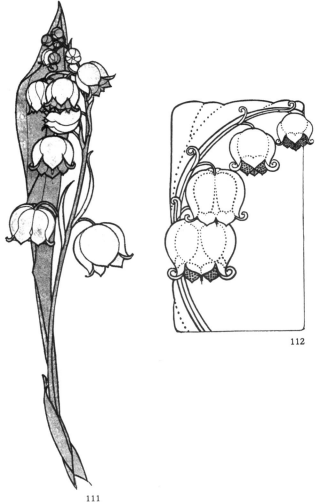

111

112

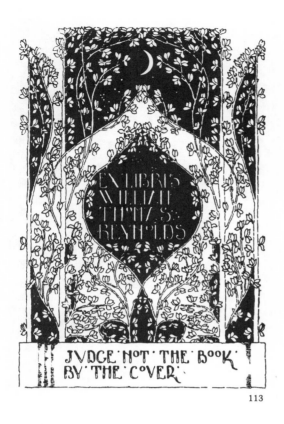

JVDGE · NOT · THE · BOOK ·
BY · THE · COVER.

113

LE
CYCLISME
PAR
J·H·ROSNY.

114

VOICES · FROM · THE · DEPTH
OF · NATURE · BORNE.

EX LIBRIS   W.B. GIBSON Sen

115

EX · W. BRUCE
LIBRIS · GIBSON

116

117

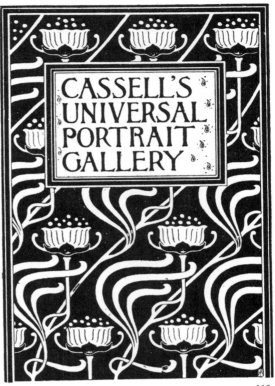

CASSELL'S UNIVERSAL PORTRAIT GALLERY

118

119

120

121

122

123

124

125

126

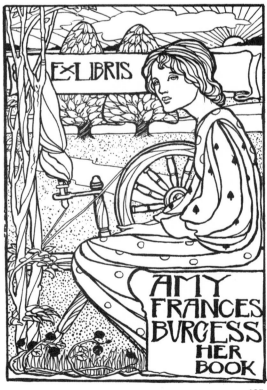

127

ART et
DÉCORATION
REVUE MENSUELLE D'ART MODERNE

A. COSSARD.

Kougeron-Vignerol sc.

128

129

130

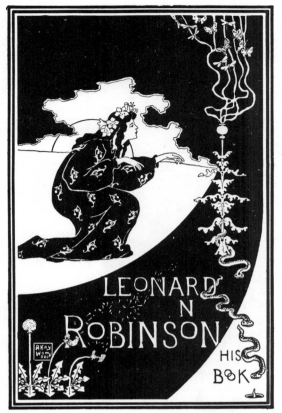

131

132

133

134

ETERNAL·HEAVENS·AGAIN ♠ TO·FEEL·ONCE·MORE·IN·PLACID·AWE·THE·STRONG·IMAGINATION·ROLL:A·SPHERE·OF·STARS·ABOVT·MY·SOVL·YEARN'D·TO·BVRST·THE·FOLDED·GLOOM:TO·BARE·THE

135

136

137

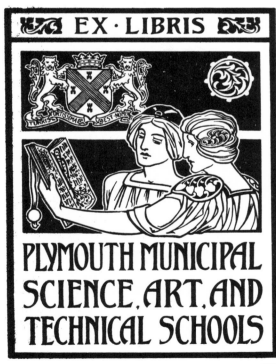

138

139

140

141

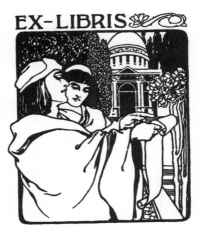

142

143

144

145

147

146

148

149

150

151

153

152

155

156

157

158

51

159

160

161

162

163

164

165

166

167

168

169

170

171

172

173

ART et DÉCORATION
Revue mensuelle illustrée d'art moderne
13, RUE LAFAYETTE . PARIS .

174

56

175

176

Her yellow hair was braided
Behind her back, a tress,
A full yard long, I guess,
And in the garden, as the Sun
uprose,
She walketh up and down,
And, as she chose,
She gathered flowers—partly
white and red—
To make a fine-woven garland
for her head;
And, as an Angel's, heavenly
was her song.

177

178

179

180

181

182

183

184

185

186

187

188

189

190

191

192

193

194

195

196

197

198

199

200

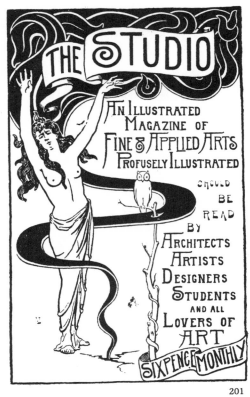

201

202

203

204

THEY · MADE · ME · THE
KEEPER · OF · THE · VINEYARDS

205

206

THE
ARCHITECTURAL · ASSOCIATION
SKETCH BOOK
THIRD SERIES Vol

EDITED BY
WILLIAM · G · B · LEWIS · AND · WILLIAM · A · PITE
⁂ LONDON ⁂
9 CONDUIT · STREET
AND
56 · GREAT · MARLBOROUGH · STREET · W
189

207

THE MOVING FINGER writes and having writ
MOVES ON: NOR ALL THY PIETY NOR WIT · · ·
· SHALL LURE IT BACK TO CANCEL HALF A LINE ·
NOR ALL THY TEARS WASH OUT A WORD OF IT ·

208

MAGIC·CASEMENTS·OPENING·ON·THE·FOAM
OF·PERILOVS·SEAS·IN·FAERY·LANDS·FORLORN

209

PEACE

210

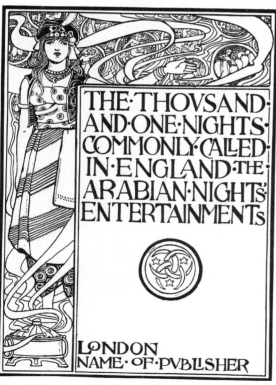

THE·THOVSAND·
AND·ONE·NIGHTS·
COMMONLY·CALLED·
IN·ENGLAND·THE·
ARABIAN·NIGHTS·
ENTERTAINMENTS

LONDON
NAME·OF·PVBLISHER

211

212

213

214

215

216

217

218

219

LA MAISON MODERNE

PARIS 82 rue des petits champs

LONDON Earls court exhibition

TORINO Esposizione internazionale d'arte decorativa moderna

MANUFACTURERS OF ALL KIND OF DECORATIVE ART

ILLUSTRATED PROSPECTUS FREE

CATALOGUE WITH 500 PHOTOS: 20 FCS credited at the first purchase of 100 FCS

220

221

222

223

224

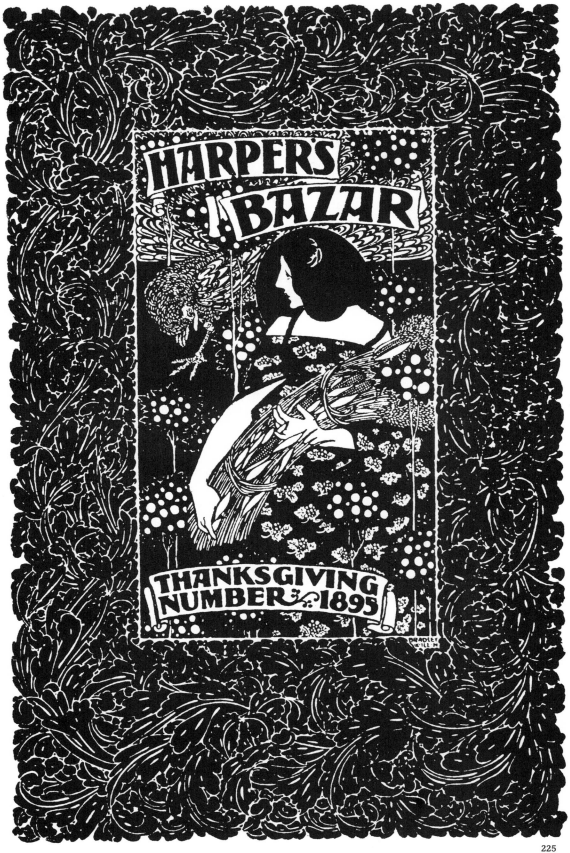

THANKSGIVING
NUMBER 1895

225

226

227

228

'LATE·LATE·SO·LATE'
FROM·TENNYSON'S·POEM

The·Novice

Guinevere

LATE, LATE, SO LATE!
AND DARK THE NIGHT
AND CHILL!
LATE, LATE, SO LATE!
BUT WE CAN ENTER
STILL!
LATE, LATE TOO LATE!
YE CANNOT ENTER
NOW!

HAVE WE NOT HEARD
THE BRIDEGROOM IS
SO SWEET?
O, LET US IN THOUGH
LATE, TO KISS HIS
FEET!
NO, NO, TOO LATE!
YE CANNOT ENTER
NOW.

NO LIGHT HAD WE:
FOR THAT WE DO
REPENT;
AND LEARNING THIS,
THE BRIDEGROOM
WILL RELENT.
TOO LATE, TOO LATE:
YE CANNOT ENTER
NOW.

NO LIGHT; SO LATE
AND DARK AND CHILL
THE NIGHT!
O, LET US IN, THAT
WE MAY FIND THE
LIGHT!
TOO LATE, TOO LATE!
YE CANNOT ENTER
NOW.

229

EX LIBRIS

230

231

232

233

ALTIOR ARDENTIOR

234

ERRAT INERRANS

235

236

237

✶NOTTVRNO✶

lionetto 1926

238

239

240

241

242

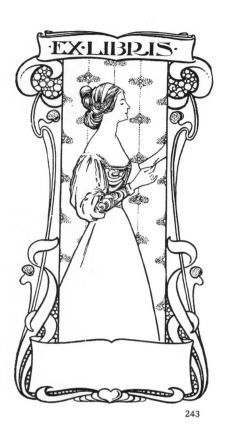

243

244

245

246

247

248

Fancy, whose various figure-
tinctured vest
Was ever changing to a dif-
ferent hue.

249

EX LIBRIS

ARTHUR
MELBOURNE
SUTTHERY

250

251

252

253

254

255

256

257

258

259

260

261

262

PER IL POSTO DI RISTORO
"LA CROCE ROSSA" DI SARZANA
"L'EROICA" DELLA SPEZIA

MOSTRA NAZIONALE D'ARTE
BIGLIETTO N°_____ L. 5.00

263

EX LIBRIS

A·TRAMBVSTI

264

EX LIBRIS
EGIDIO CORA

265

266

267

268

269

270

271

272

273

274

275

276

277

278

279

280

281

282

283

284

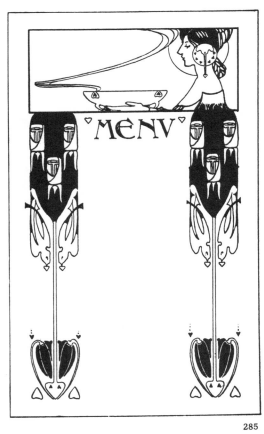

285

286

287

288

289

290

291

292

293

294

295

296

297

MENU

298

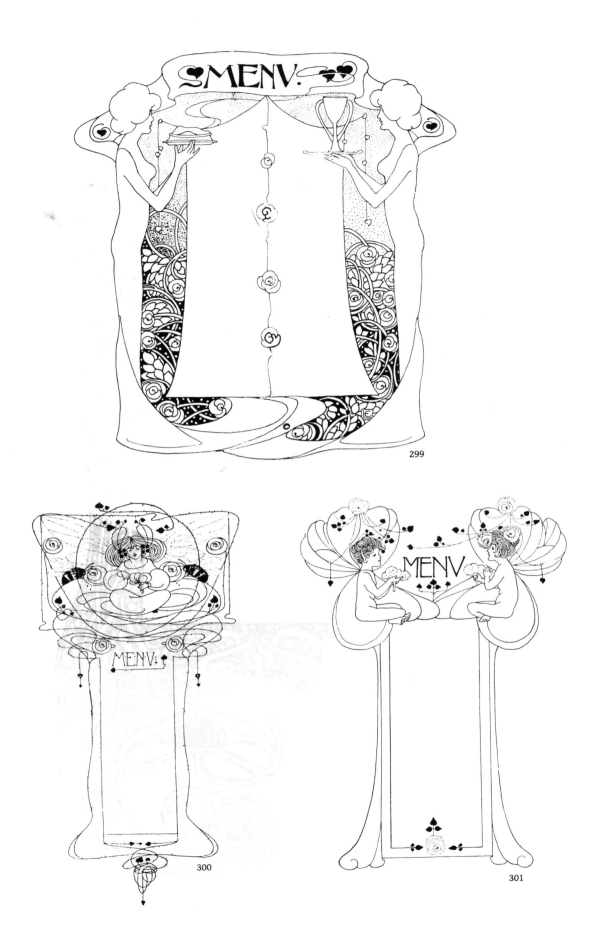

299

300

301

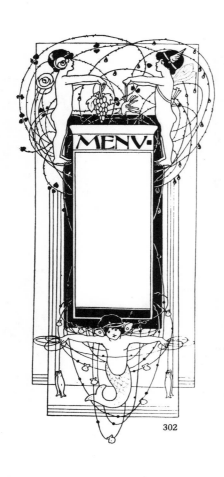

302

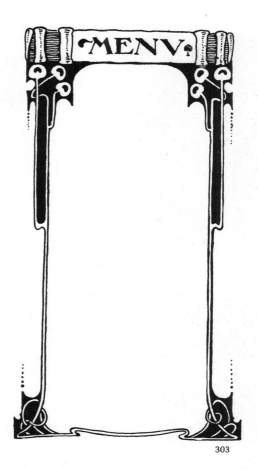

303

304

305

306

307

308

309

310

311

312

313

314

315

316

317

318

319

320

321

322

323

324

325

326

327

328

329

330

331

332

333

334

335

338

336

337

339

340

341

342

343

344

345

346

347

348

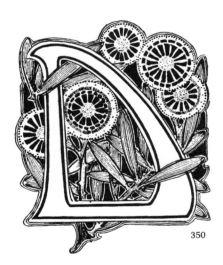

349

350

351

352

353

354

355

356

357

358

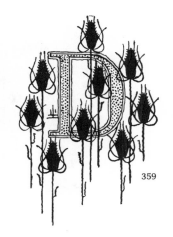

359

360

361

362

363

364

365

366

367

368

369

370

371

372

373

374

375

376

378

379

377

380

381

382

383

384

385

386

387

388

389

390

391

392

393

394

395

400

393

396

397

398

399

401

402

403

404

405

406

407

408

409

410

411

412

413

414

415

416

417

418

419

420

421

422

423

424

425

426

427

428

429

430

431

432

433

434

435

436

437

438

439

440

441

442

443

444

445

446

447

448

104

449

450

451

452

453

454

455

456

457

458

459

460

461

462

463

464

465

466

467

468

469

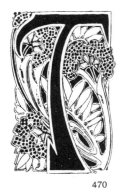

470

471

472

473

474

475

476

477

478

479

480

481

482

483

484

485

486

487

488

489

490

491

492

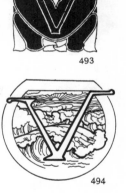

493

494

495

496

497

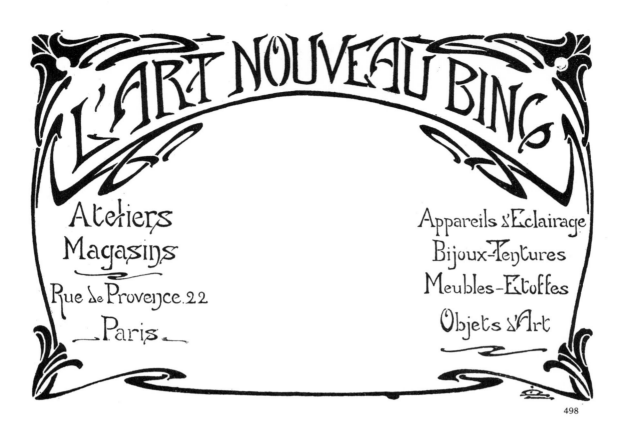

498

499

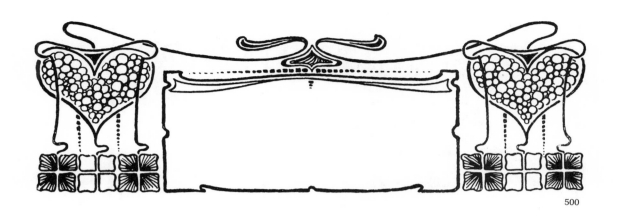

500

L'ART DANS L'HABITATION
G. SERRURIER

PARIS 54 RUE DE TOCQUEVILLE.
BRUXELLES 21 RUE DE LA BLANCHISSERIE.
LIÈGE 39 RUE HEMRICOURT.

EXPOSITION PERMANENTE D'INTE=
=RIEURS MODERNES COMPLETE=
=MENT MEUBLES DECORES ET OR=
=NES SALONS. SALLES A
MANGER. CHAMBRES A COUCHER.
CABINETS DE TRAVAIL. ANTICHAM=
=BRES. ETC MISE EN OEU=
=VRE ET ADAPTATION RATIONNELLE
DE TOUS LES MATERIAUX ET PRO=
=DUITS DE L'INDUSTRIE MODERNE.

501

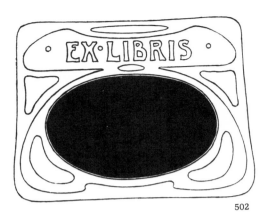

502

503

Eugène   Belville

504

505

506

507

508

509

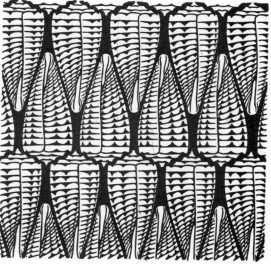

510

511

512

513

514

515

516

517

518

519

520

521

522

523

116

524

525

117

LE VIE DELL'ARIA

526

IL·PROBLEMA·DELLA
·RICOSTRVZIONE·NEI·PAESI·DEVASTATI
DALLA·GVERRA

527

528

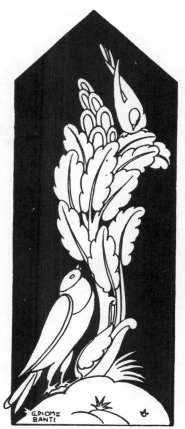

529

530

531

Le Progrès Agricole.

Organe agricole et horticole de la région du Nord,
paraissant le Dimanche.
Écrire pour le laboureur c'est faire l'aumône au pauvre.
J. Bujault.

Directeur
Georges Raquet.

532

EX-LIBRIS

533

THE SCOTTISH MUSICAL REVIEW:

534

THE STU-DIO

535

536

537

538

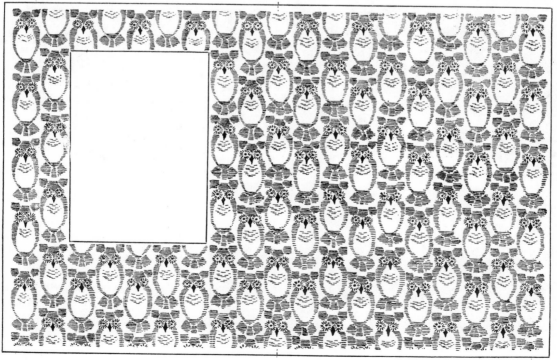

539

121

FRATELLI·GRIMM
L'UCCELLO·D'ORO

540

541

542

543

EX LIBRIS LOUIS DUNTON

544

19 07

GREAT MEN TALK TO US IN GOOD BOOKS

EX·LIBRIS

545

EX LIBRIS.

HANS VOLKERT

546

THE STUDIO

547

548

549

LITTLE MISS MUFFIT.

550

551

552

553

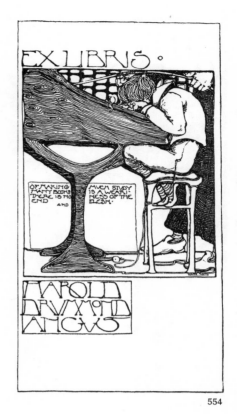

554

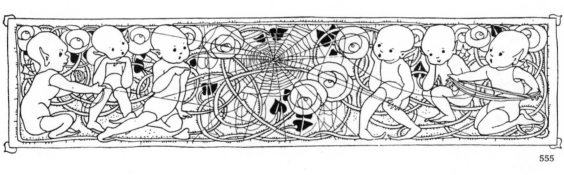

555

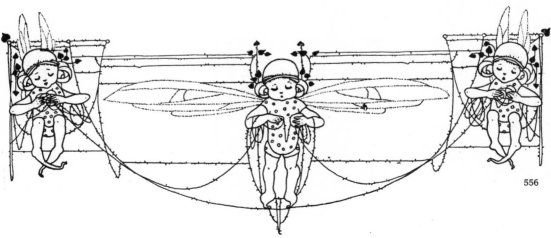

556

AUTUMN

557

CHAPTER I.

558

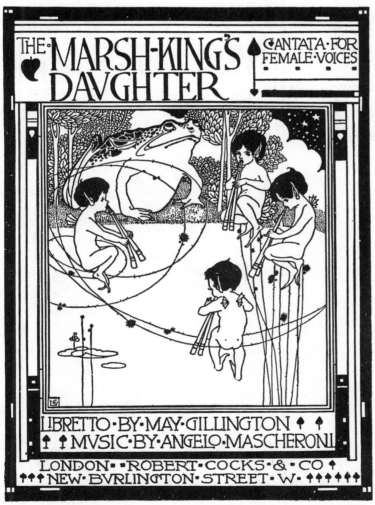

THE MARSH-KING'S DAVGHTER
CANTATA FOR FEMALE VOICES

LIBRETTO BY MAY GILLINGTON
MVSIC BY ANGELO MASCHERONI
LONDON ROBERT COCKS & CO
NEW BVRLINGTON STREET W

559

FROM AMONG THE BOOKS OF

JEANNE JARDINIER

560

129

561

EX LIBRIS

Marjory Leon Stoatley Rough

562

EX LIBRIS
S.H.HEATH

563

WALTER H BRACKETT

READING MAK-
-ETH A FULL MAN

564

THE CHILDS FAIRY TALE BOOK

565

566

567

568

569

570

571

LVCY·LOCKET·LOST·HER·POCKET·
KITTY·FISHER·FOUND·IT·
THERE·WAS·NOT·A·PENNY·IN·IT·
BUT·A·RIBBON·ROUND·IT

572

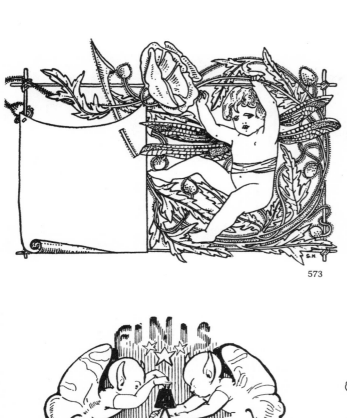

573

574

575

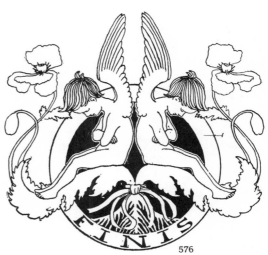

576

577

Identification of Artists
and Sources of Illustrations

This list identifies, wherever possible, the artist responsible for each illustration and the source in which the illustration originally appeared. With regard to illustrations from *The Studio*, discrepancies between the signatures on the pictures themselves and the identifications below are attributable to that publication's practice of conducting pseudonymous design competitions within its pages. Immediately following is a bibliography of sources used in this collection, with the abbreviations to be used in the citations following the bibliography.

Gli Adornatori del Libro in Italia (Bologna, Italy: 1923–27). (*Adornatori*)
Art et Décoration (Paris: 1897–1911). (*Art*)
Holme, Geoffrey. *British Book Illustration Yesterday and To-day* (London: The Studio, 1923). (*British*)
Ratta, Cesare. *L'Arte del Libro e della Rivista nei Paesi d'Europa e d'America* (Bologna, Italy: 1925, 1928). (*L'Arte*)
The Studio (London: 1894–1920). (*Studio*)

Frontispiece: Thomas Henry, *Studio* 10.
Copyright page: *Art*.
1. *Art*.
2. Ernst Koie, *Studio* 14.
3. Edgar Wilson, *Studio* 4.
4. Leonard Brooke, *Studio* 43.
5. Leonard Brooke, *Studio* 42.
6. *Art*.
7. George Auriol, *Studio* 47.
8 & 9. *Art*.
10. Percy Lancaster, *Studio* 27.
11. Ethel Larcombe, *Studio* 27.
12. G. W. Mason, *Studio* 27.
13 & 14. Charles Ricketts, *Studio* 4.
15. *Art*.
16. F. D. Watts, *Studio* 39.
17. George Auriol.
18. C. F. A. Voysey, *Studio* 1.
19. *Art*.
20. Eugène Grasset, *Studio* 4.
21. C. H. B. Quennell, *Studio* 10.
22. Arthur Silver, *Studio* 3.
23. Marie Jacounchikoff, *Studio* 10.
24. Koloman Moser, *Studio* 33.
25. Arthur Silver, *Studio* 3.
26. *Art*.
27. Ernst Aufseeser, *Studio* 61.
28–30. *Art*.
31. Agnes C. Martin, *Studio* 7.
32. Isabel Haddon, *Studio* 12.
33. George Marples, *Studio* 7.
34. *Art*.
35. Mary L. Goodacre, *Studio* 7.
37. Josef M. Auchentaller.
40. Alfred Bohm.
41. Josef M. Auchentaller.
42 & 43. Ethel Larcombe, *Studio* 28.
44–48. *Art*.
49. H. C. Graff, *Studio* 5.
50. *Art*.
51 & 52. Gleeson White, *Studio* 4.
53. Florence Phillips, *Studio* 5.
54. J. G. Hardy, *Studio* 5.

55. Bruno Seuchter, *Studio* 39.
56. Beatrice M. Gower, *Studio* 51.
57. James A. Found, *Studio* 51.
58. J. I. Kay, *Studio* 2.
59–62. *Art*.
63. *Adornatori*.
64. E. Romagnoli, *L'Arte*.
65. *L'Arte*.
66. Eugène Grasset, *L'Arte*.
67. Paolo Bevilacqua, *L'Arte*.
68. Sophie Pumphrey, *Studio* 3.
69. Granville Fell, *Studio* 4.
70. John J. Crook, *Studio* 38.
71. E. W. Wimperis, *Studio* 3.
72. Ethel Larcombe, *Studio* 28.
73. *Studio* 2.
74. Mary Thomas, *Studio* 28.
75. E. Ransom, *Studio* 2.
76–78. *Art*.
80. Marguèrite Igglesden, *Studio* 28.
81. *Studio* 17.
82. May Dixon, *Studio* 1.
83. J. Illingworth Kay, *Studio* 1.
84. *Art*.
85. C. H. B. Quennell, *Studio* 10.
86. Alex. Allen Foote, *Studio* 40.
87. Alfred Dennis, *Studio* 12.
88. F. C. Tilney, *Studio* 4.
89. R. C. West, *Studio* 30.
90. Ethel Larcombe, *Studio* 30.
91. Lionel A. Bowen, *Studio* 30.
92. Lennox G. Bird, *Studio* 30.
93. Oswald Dittrich, *Studio* 39.
94. E. Fromel, *Studio* 39.
95. James Guthrie, *Studio* 61.
96. Ethel Larcombe, *Studio* 22.
97. Ronald Simpson, *Studio* 84.
99. Howard Stringer, *Studio* 5.
100. Talwin Morris, *Studio* 15.
101. Herbert Dobby, *Studio* 8.
102. Talwin Morris, *Studio* 15.
103. Dardo Battaglini, *Adornatori*.
104. A. Laager, *L'Arte*.

105. E. Berchmens, *L'Arte*.
106. Guido Marussig, *Adornatori*.
107. Dardo Battaglini, *Adornatori*.
108. George Auriol, *Studio* 61.
109 & 110. *Art*.
111 & 112. *Studio* 54.
113. Paget L. Baxter, *Studio* 3.
114. *Art*.
115 & 116. W. Bruce Gibson, *Studio* 3.
119 & 120. *Adornatori*.
121. Ronald Simpson, *Studio* 84.
122. James Guthrie, *Studio* 84.
123. Ethel Larcombe, *Studio* 22.
124 & 125. Arthur Maude, *Studio* 7.
126. Eugène Grasset, *Studio* 4.
127. Ethel Kate Burgess, *Studio* 10.
128. A. Cossard, *Art*.
129. C. A. Walker, *Studio* 11.
130. Evelyn Holden, *Studio* 7.
131. A. K. Womrath, *Studio* 10.
132. R. Anning Bell, *Studio* 4.
133. A. K. Womrath, *Studio* 10.
134. Ethel Larcombe, *Studio* 32.
135. Ethel Larcombe, *Studio* 30.
136 & 137. Ethel Larcombe, *Studio* 27.
138. E. R. Phillips, *Studio* 27.
139. Dorothy M. Payne, *Studio* 50.
140. W. E. Webster, *Studio* 12.
141. Ethel Larcombe, *Studio* 38.
142. Fred H. Ball, *Studio* 40.
143. J. Walter West, *Studio* 6.
144. *Art*.
145. Maurice DeLambert, *Studio* 19.
146. James A. Found, *Studio* 22.
147. Ethel Larcombe, *Studio* 20.
149. J. Walter West, *Studio* 5.
152. Thomas Parsons, *Studio* 40.
153. Ellen E. Houghton, *Studio* 15.
154. John Austen, *British*.
155. Hans Volkert.
156. Fred Hyland.
157. Hans Christiansen.
158. E. M. Lilien.

159. Alfred Roller.
161. Gustav Klimt.
162 & 163. *Art.*
164. W. B. McDougall, *Studio* 7.
167. R. Anning Bell, *Studio* 2.
168. Ethel Larcombe, *Studio* 21.
169. Ethel Larcombe, *Studio* 22.
170. Scott Calder, *Studio* 10.
171. *Art.*
172. Koloman Moser, *Studio* 33.
173. M. Fernie, *Studio* 5.
174. *Art.*
175. *Studio* 37.
176. Harold Nelson, *Studio* 46.
177. D. Chamberlain, *Studio* 11.
178. *Art.*
179. Ethel Larcombe, *Studio* 27.
180. Fred H. Ball, *Studio* 37.
181. A. M. Dell, *Studio* 31.
182. Dorothy M. Payne, *Studio* 50.
183. Winifred L. Stamp, *Studio* 35.
184. Fred H. Ball, *Studio* 12.
185. J. Walter West, *Studio* 10.
186. Grace M. McClure, *Studio* 27.
187. Fred H. Ball, *Studio* 48.
188. Fred H. Ball, *Studio* 26.
189. Fred H. Ball, *Studio* 27.
190. Charles Robinson, *Studio* 6.
191. Giovanni Mataloni, *L'Arte.*
192. Publio Morbiducci, *L'Arte.*
193. Guido Marussig, *Adornatori.*
194. Giovanni Mataloni, *L'Arte.*
195. Carlo D'Aloisio, *Adornatori.*
196. Giovanni Fumagalli, *L'Arte.*
197. Emilio Mantelli, *L'Arte.*
198. *Adornatori.*
199. Giovanni Mataloni, *L'Arte.*
200. Joan Bell, *Studio* 28.
201. C. T. Prescott, *Studio* 2.
202. Will Bradley, *Studio* 4.
204. Percy Lancaster, *Studio* 38.
205. Margaret Thompson, *Studio* 15.
206. Fernand Khnopff, *Studio* 2.
207. Osmund M. Pittmann, *Studio* 14.
208. Fred H. Ball, *Studio* 42.
209. Fred H. Ball, *Studio* 40.
210. Mary S. Tyrer, *Studio* 17.
211. Ethel Larcombe, *Studio* 19.
212. Leon V. Solon, *Studio* 31.
213. J. Christofferson, *L'Arte.*
214. Carlo D'Aloisio, *Adornatori.*
215 & 216. *Adornatori.*
217. Paolo Paschetto, *L'Arte.*
218. R. Anning Bell, *Studio* 52.
219. Anna Dixon, *Studio* 22.
220. Maurice Bais, *Art.*
221 & 223. Harold Nelson, *Studio* 73.
224. Winifred L. Stamp, *Studio* 35.
225. Will Bradley, *L'Arte.*
226. Carlo D'Aloisio, *Adornatori.*
227. Giovanni Fumagalli, *Adornatori.*
228. E. L. Appleby, *Studio* 4.
229. Gertrude Lindsay, *Studio* 21.
230. R. Anning Bell, *Studio* 3.
231. Alice Maud Fabian, *Studio* 12.
232. Harold Nelson, *Studio* 19.
233. Norman Ault, *Studio* 21.
234-237. Antonello Moroni, *L'Arte.*
238. Lionella Nasi, *Adornatori.*
239. A. Scott Carter, *Studio* 27.
240. M. F. Verneuil, *Art.*

241. Isobel B. Williamson, *Studio* 11.
242. Edith Richardson, *Studio* 7.
243. Percy Lancaster, *Studio* 27.
244. E. H. Swinstead, *Studio* 27.
245. Janet S. C. Simpson, *Studio* 20.
246. Lilian Crabb, *Studio* 29.
247. Lilian Rusbridge, *Studio* 26.
248. *Studio* 4.
249. Gwynedd M. Hudson, *Studio* 40.
250. R. Anning Bell, *Studio* 3.
251. Osmund M. Pittmann, *Studio* 18.
252. Thomas A. Cook, *Studio* 39.
253. Ethel Larcombe, *Studio* 46.
254. Ethel M. Raeburn, *Studio* 6.
255 & 256. A. W. Dodd, *Studio* 34.
257. Ida F. Ravaison, *Studio* 17.
258. Olive Allen, *Studio* 17.
259. Harry Clarke, *Studio* 78.
260 & 261. Giovanni Fumagalli, *Adornatori.*
263. Enrico Mantelli, *L'Arte.*
264 & 265. Giovanni Mataloni, *L'Arte.*
266 & 267. Harold Nelson, *Studio* 19.
268. Herbert P. Horner, *Studio* 2.
269. Alma C. Smedley, *Studio* 7.
270. R. P. Gossop, *Studio* 26.
272. Maurice DeLambert, *Studio* 19.
273. Harold Nelson, *Studio* 63.
274. Ethel Larcombe, *Studio* 22.
275. *Art.*
277. Walter Frank Vernon Anson, *Studio* 53.
278. Peter C. Brown, *Studio* 2.
279. Stavros Homere, *Studio* 7.
280. Thomas Frost, *Studio* 30.
281. Violet M. Holden, *Studio* 2.
282. George M. Ellwood, *Studio* 11.
283 & 284. Ethel Larcombe, *Studio* 23.
285. T. A. Cook, *Studio* 29.
286. Oswald Schwemmer, *Studio* 35.
287. Fred H. Ball, *Studio* 29.
288. Fred H. Ball, *Studio* 35.
289. Ethel Larcombe, *Studio* 25.
290. John J. Crook, *Studio* 29.
291-297. *Art.*
298. John J. Crook, *Studio* 29.
299. Ethel Larcombe, *Studio* 25.
300. Ethel Larcombe, *Studio* 29.
301. Ethel Larcombe, *Studio* 25.
302. Ethel Larcombe, *Studio* 29.
304. George Halford, *Studio* 35.
305. A. M. Burleigh, *Studio* 35.
306. G. F. Burton, *Studio* 25.
307. *Art.*
308-312. *Art.*
313. Ethel Larcombe, *Studio* 33.
314. Gertrude E. Stevens, *Studio* 25.
315. J. L. Ward, *Studio* 21.
316. Jacques Bonnier, *Studio* 49.
317. W. A. Burton, *Studio* 33.
318. Winifred Christie, *Studio* 33.
319. M. A. Massie, *Studio* 49.
320 & 321. *Art.*
322. J. R. Lang, *Studio* 25.
323-326. *Art.*
327. E. G. Hallam, *Studio* 33.
328. Fred H. Ball, *Studio* 25.
329. S. C. McKean, *Studio* 25.
330. Jacques Bonnier, *Studio* 49.
331. Elsie M. Henderson, *Studio* 25.
332. Jessie D. Meech, *Studio* 21.

333. *Art.*
334. L. Fuchs, *Art.*
335. G. F. Burton, *Studio* 33.
336 & 337. *Art.*
338. E. G. Hallam, *Studio* 33.
339. C. M. Hibbs, *Studio* 33.
340. *Art.*
341. Ivy Millicent James, *Studio* 21.
342-345. *Art.*
346. Alfred C. Hooker, *Studio* 49.
347. Mrs. William Chance, *Studio* 21.
348. Jacques Bonnier, *Studio* 49.
349. G. W. Mason, *Studio* 49.
350 & 351. *Art.*
352. C. M. Hibbs, *Studio* 33.
353. Chris. Ambler, *Studio* 49.
354. H. G. Spooner, *Studio* 33.
355. Leonard Brooke, *Studio* 49.
356. Jacques Bonnier, *Studio* 49.
357-361. *Art.*
362. Leonard Brooke, *Studio* 49.
363. Winifred Christie, *Studio* 33.
364. *Art.*
365. Chris. Ambler, *Studio* 49.
366. May M. Falcon, *Studio* 21.
367-369. *Art.*
370. Jacques Bonnier, *Studio* 49.
371 & 372. *Art.*
373. Ethel Larcombe, *Studio* 33.
374. May M. Falcon, *Studio* 21.
375. *Art.*
376. W. A. Burton, *Studio* 33.
377. E. G. Hallam, *Studio* 33.
378 & 379. *Art.*
380. May M. Falcon, *Studio* 21.
381-385. *Art.*
386. Winifred Christie, *Studio* 33.
387. Leonard Brooke, *Studio* 49.
388. M. A. Massie, *Studio* 49.
389. *Art.*
390. Ivy Millicent James, *Studio* 21.
391. Chris. Ambler, *Studio* 49.
392-396. *Art.*
397. C. M. Hibbs, *Studio* 33.
398-417. *Art.*
418. Ivy Millicent James, *Studio* 21.
419 & 420. *Art.*
421. *Studio* 25.
422. W. A. Burton, *Studio* 33.
423. *Art.*
424. Ethel Larcombe, *Studio* 33.
425. Salomo Birnbaum, *Studio* 49.
426. Winifred Christie, *Studio* 33.
427. G. F. Burton, *Studio* 33.
428-430. *Art.*
431. M. A. Massie, *Studio* 49.
432. *Art.*
433. May M. Falcon, *Studio* 21.
434. *Art.*
435. Charles E. Cundall, *Studio* 49.
436. Leonard Brooke, *Studio* 49.
437. M. A. Massie, *Studio* 49.
438. H. G. Spooner, *Studio* 33.
439. E. G. Hallam, *Studio* 33.
440. *Art.*
441. C. M. Hibbs, *Studio* 33.
442-447. *Art.*
448. G. F. Burton, *Studio* 33.
449. Winifred Christie, *Studio* 33.
450. Ethel Larcombe, *Studio* 33.
451. Th. Burrot, *Studio* 49.

452. G. F. Burton, *Studio* 33.
453. W. A. Burton, *Studio* 33.
454. Ida A. Ravaison, *Studio* 25.
455 & 456. *Art.*
457. Chris. Ambler, *Studio* 49.
458. H. G. Spooner, *Studio* 33.
459. May M. Falcon, *Studio* 21.
460. E. G. Hallam, *Studio* 33.
461. *Art.*
462. C. M. Hibbs, *Studio* 33.
463. Leonard Brooke, *Studio* 49.
464. *Art.*
465. Edith Mary Fry, *Studio* 49.
466. M. A. Massie, *Studio* 49.
467. Ethel Larcombe, *Studio* 33.
468. *Art.*
469. Winifred Christie, *Studio* 33.
470-472. *Art.*
473. Leonard Brooke, *Studio* 49.
474 & 475. *Art.*
476. Katharine Richardson, *Studio* 25.
477. E. G. Bareham, *Studio* 33.
478. E. G. Hallam, *Studio* 33.
479. M. A. Massie, *Studio* 49.
480. May M. Falcon, *Studio* 21.
481. Ivy Millicent James, *Studio* 21.
482. *Art.*
483. W. A. Burton, *Studio* 33.
484. H. G. Spooner, *Studio* 33.
485. Muriel C. Ridley, *Studio* 49.
486-488. *Art.*
489. Leonard Brooke, *Studio* 49.
490. Ivy Millicent James, *Studio* 21.
491. Chris. Ambler, *Studio* 49.
492. *Art.*

493. G. F. Burton, *Studio* 33.
494. *Art.*
495. Ivy Millicent James, *Studio* 21.
496. Jeanne Plateau, *Studio* 49.
497. G. F. Burton, *Studio* 33.
498 & 499. *Art.*
500. Percy Lancaster, *Studio* 26.
501. *Art.*
502. Lucy Renouf, *Studio* 30.
503. Scott Calder, *Studio* 40.
504. *Art.*
505. C. K. Cook, *Studio* 39.
511. F. Thibaut, *Studio* 28.
512. C. J. Beese, *Studio* 28.
513. Giovanni Fumagalli, *Adornatori.*
514. Dardo Battaglini, *L'Arte.*
515. Antonello Moroni, *L'Arte.*
516. *Adornatori.*
517. Carlo D'Aloisio, *Adornatori.*
518 & 519. *Adornatori.*
521. Albert E. Oldham, *Studio* 32.
522. Ethel Larcombe, *Studio* 23.
523. James Hall, *Studio* 43.
524 & 525. T. Allwork Chaplin, *Studio* 32.
526 & 527. Guido Marussig, *Adornatori.*
528-531. G. Piombanti, *Adornatori.*
532. *Art.*
533. Svante Olsson, *Studio* 27.
534. C. R. Mackintosh, *Studio* 11.
535. Lydia Skottsberg, *Studio* 18.
536. Harold Nelson, *Studio* 4.
538. H. Brockhurst, *Studio* 39.
539. Marguèrite Igglesden, *Studio* 28.
540. Dario Betti, *L'Arte.*

541. Giovanni Fumagalli, *Adornatori.*
542 & 543. V. Venturini, *Adornatori.*
544. E. G. Perman, *Studio* 27.
545. John A. Chell, *Studio* 40.
546. H. Volkert, *Studio* 34.
547. Miss E. Francis, *Studio* 42.
549. Jeanne A. Larousse, *Studio* 73.
550. T. Allwork Chaplin, *Studio* 32.
551 & 552. Chris. Ambler, *Studio* 48.
553. Olive Allen, *Studio* 19.
554. Olive Allen, *Studio* 20.
555. Ethel Larcombe, *Studio* 37.
556. Ethel Larcombe, *Studio* 39.
557. Evelyn Holden, *Studio* 5.
558. Maurice Clifford, *Studio* 12.
559. Ethel Larcombe, *Studio* 35.
560. Olive Allen, *Studio* 22.
561. Dorothy M. Payne, *Studio* 50.
562. Miss Aberigh-MacKay, *Studio* 20.
563. Sidney Heath, *Studio* 1.
564. Oliver Brackett, *Studio* 2.
565. Ethel K. Burgess, *Studio* 11.
566. C. M. Gere, *Studio* 2.
567. L. J. Ward, *Studio* 20.
568. Jessie Mitchell, *Studio* 7.
569. Claire Murrell, *Studio* 22.
570. Ethel Larcombe, *Studio* 26.
571. Ethel Larcombe, *Studio* 23.
572. Ethel Larcombe, *Studio* 32.
573. Sidney Heath, *Studio* 1.
574. V. and E. Holden, *Studio* 6.
575. F. Kirk Shaw, *Studio* 48.
576. Marion Wallace-Dunlop, *Studio* 12.
577. Gwynedd Palin, *Studio* 12.